AF255810

Emancipation

Emancipation

Charlotte Lynn Hultquist

RESOURCE *Publications* · Eugene, Oregon

Resource Publications
An Imprint of Wipf and Stock Publishers
199 W. 8th Ave., Suite 3
Eugene, OR 97401

www.wipfandstock.com

PAPERBACK ISBN: 978-1-6667-8258-5
HARDCOVER ISBN: 978-1-6667-8259-2
EBOOK ISBN: 978-1-6667-8260-8

06/28/23

Dedication

This collection is dedicated to the wonderful people of Our Savior Lutheran Church. Most of these poems began as little seedlings that I found during the beautiful liturgy and our conversations outside of church. After being diagnosed with PTSD from religious abuse and spiritual trauma, I didn't know if I could survive a church service. God drew me to you in the bleakest of times, when I had a child in the Covid ICU and didn't know where to turn for consolation or prayer. The words of Scripture were weaponized and bent into crooked misrepresentations before I met you, but you held up the shining, grace-filled Word without sharp edges. For the first year, I wept into my required face mask every time Pastor Kyle dipped his hand into the water bowl and raised it, proclaiming that we are forgiven. My soul has been washed and healed every Sunday. When PTSD triggers reared up at Christian words and ideas, I found my nervous system wonderfully grounded by your grace-filled, peaceful presence. You have ushered my children and me into a sane, steadfast faith without any cognitive dissonance or punishing wrath. We will always love you!

Contents

Let Them Go

Emancipation | 2
Scapegoat | 4
The Crash | 5
Escape | 7
Marriage Journey | 8
Grit | 10
Religious Abuse | 11
Hypervigilance | 12
Abdication | 13
Paranoia | 15

The Unraveling

Weary | 18
Mirror | 19
Still Here | 20
Sometimes Grief | 21
Losing or Keeping | 22
Rag Doll | 23
In the Earth | 24
Is Life Harder Now? | 25

Build a New Normal

Always in My Hands | 28
Worth the Pain? | 29
Shunned | 31
Dear Suffering | 32
The Strong One | 34
Asher | 35
Peripheral Neuropathy | 37
Book Choices | 38
Read Aloud Time | 39
Crochet Therapy | 41
Enigma | 42
Solid Ground | 43
Security | 44
Anthony | 45
Long Covid | 46
My Heart | 47

Let Them Go

*Learning to drift away from
where I was born*

Emancipation

Little girl, don't you believe
her heap of lies about this world.
It's not the minefield she depicts;
she's hoodwinked by her fears.
You're gonna shed those lies like skin,
you'll outgrow them one by one
when the fears lose all their value
and her words stop ringing true.

It's convenient for her now
to fix these strings on you,
the cobwebs of deception
and the apron strings of shame.
You'll submit and think it's holy,
she'll commend you for your love
until you break the cords that tangle,
leaving her to clean her mess.

Then you'll find your legs are solid,
you're not pitiful or frail.
You weren't spineless, just deluded
by her crocodile tears.
She's affronted and resentful
but somehow you keep your cool.
Her choleric disposition can't
constrain you anymore.

Unbeknownst to those who hold you
there's a strength beneath your feet.
Roots and sinew plunging downward,
ever downward, drinking deep
of ancient lakes of wisdom.
She can't play you anymore.
The depth of sinew isn't seen but felt
When you escape.

Scapegoat

Soul sinking
Plunging into
Caverns deep
Great despair

Punished for the
Sins of others
Handy scapegoat
Little lamb

Unjust treatment
At the hands of
One you try to
Show your love

Opens caverns
Endless questions
Other women
Never ask

Labeled crazy
And ungrateful
Should I thank you
For your "love"

The Crash

I lived in a land
Of nonsense and farce
Mystical, magical
Untethered to the solid earth
A land on God's board game
Maneuvered by his hand
According to our tresspasses
And his chaotic moods

I peered down below
At those on solid ground
Deceived, depraved
Unfettered by religion's cords
A land on fertile soil
Choosing and building
According to their instincts
Not God's chaotic moods

They warned me of monsters
Of demons and torment
Mystical, magical
Untethered to the natural
A land to catch jumpers
Maneuvered by the devil's hand
According to their copious sins
And his chaotic moods

I dove off the board game
Labeled heretic and fraud
Deceived, depraved
Unfettered by religion's cords
Toward the fertile soil
Choosing to risk torment
According to wild doubts
About God's chaotic moods

I shattered on impact
That was the goal
Regenerate, renew
Untethered to religion
A land of independence
Maneuvered by my hands
According to my preference
And my human moods

Escape

Squirm, stretch
Writhe, groan
Discomfort is constant
Cords tangle round
Smile, frown
Nod, bend
All of us bound up
No one is free

Look, listen
Yearn, reach
Discomfort won't stop me
Push through the pain
Moan, cry
Shove, sweat
Trust in your instincts
Freedom is real

Dream, sigh
Search, hope
Protest and question
Sever the cords
Burns, sores
Blood, tears
Run while exhausted
Never look back

Marriage Journey

The journey we're on
Is a literal road
Three miles of pavement
Our feet touch each day

Each mile rubs off
Dirt from our souls
As dirt cakes onto
The soles of our shoes

Unpredictable marriage
All brambles and thorns
Anvils keep falling
Stale food, broken home

A bend in the road
Once distant, now close
No signs to show
If a fork is ahead

The turn might be hiding
A smooth path of grass
Fruit on lush bushes
Comfort and peace

Or it may conceal
Narrow stone paths
Where wise, healthy people
Part ways with good will

Can I walk with you
All the way to that turn
Step into its curve
And look beyond

My heart is screaming
Don't take the risk
Authentic life isn't
Worth such pain

Impossible for us
To feel peace now
Unless we turn there
Truth costs so much

I love you enough
That I want to stop here
And I love you enough
To never stop here

I love me enough
To stay in half darkness
And I love me enough
To step toward full light

Grit

There's a strength
that only grows
in those
who are buried
and dig their way out.

You know the darkness
grimmer than night
haze and fog
when you're buried
but dig your way out.

You know the whisper
enticing and clear
"No escape
when you're buried,"
but dig your way out.

You know a burden
of leaden shadows
that oppress
when you're buried,
but dig your way out.

You know the delight
of emancipation
sigh and stretch
you were buried,
but dug your way out.

Religious Abuse

Cringe inward
Gasp with alarm
The man of god
Proclaims the bad news

God is watching
Disappointed, stern
Shaking his head
You don't make the grade

Liquid regret
Sorrow and heartbreak
You creep even deeper
Into your cave

Visceral shame
Prickles your spine
Humanity's stench
Your heinous problem

Dreadful knowledge
Becomes more certain
Even your good works
Are filthy rags

Hypervigilance

Tiptoe
Creep past
Hold my breath
You're a ticking bomb
The slightest move
Makes you explode

Tiptoe
Creep past
Bite my tongue
You're a glass cup
The wrong noise
Makes you shatter

Tiptoe
Creep past
Choke my tears
You're the West Witch
The liquid emotion
Makes you melt down

Will you
Creep past
Bite your tongue
Become concerned
For harming the one
Who comforted you?

Abdication

The intangible thing in a person
That makes him the person he is
Is generally firm in that person
First breath to final hushed gasp.

How then did it float away from him?
Where did his soul find escape?
The trauma was deep like an ocean;
The grief like a tidal wave came.

Two deaths, situations so different,
Two blows cut the same deep gauge.
His soul, just a fragment already,
Crumpled below the great loss.

Was his soul swept away in the tumult?
Are the pieces still somewhere inside?
That soul which I loved so deeply;
All my love melted off it like wax.

You think that death is the ending
To be feared above all else,
The most painful way of losing
Someone you trust and adore.

Far worse is losing while living,
This eerie nightmare without morn,
Losing his essence but seeing
The body that once was its home.

Somehow I survived
When his soul disappeared.

Paranoia

Why can't you see?
Standing with me
Hear the words
Watch the scene
Lost on you
Fog in your mind
Obscures reality
Still you rage at me
When I act
According
To reality
Reason flusters you
Evidence angers you
Compassion frightens you
Finally
I step
Away

The Unraveling

*Life falls apart while I'm
put back together*

Weary

Drag your weary limbs
Through another afternoon
Knowing that he's coming home
Knowing he's still himself

Drag your weary mind
Through another evening
Knowing his lies will strike deep
Knowing he's crafted more today

Drag your weary heart
Through another night
Knowing he can't look at you
Knowing he chokes with disgust

Drag your weary spirit
Through another dawn
Knowing he holds the blindfold
Knowing you must wear it

Darling, drag yourself away
A musty cave is better
Than living with him like this
Drag yourself to freedom

The Mirror

Staring at the mirror
It can't lie
Or can it?
He says I'm too ugly
He can't hear what I'm saying
Because the words emerge
From a hideous face
I'm telling him again
That I need his help

Staring at the mirror
It can't lie
But is it?
Two eyes, hazel blue
Pale skin, nice and smooth
This hideous face
Seems normal to me
But he wouldn't lie
Must be the mirror

Still Here

I didn't realize
The world was still here
The places I loved
Where I found solace
Where I passed happy days
Before he snatched me
I thought they disintegrated
Blew away in the storm
What a joy to see them
When I've escaped
They waited for me
They didn't feel that storm
It only hit me

Sometimes Grief

Sometimes grief
Drips down
All day long
A ceaseless flow
But very slight
Leaky sink dripping
Evidence of an
Emotional flood
Hides under covers
In soggy bed
The tears that come
Mere residue
From deeper source
Easy to hide
Harder to carry
Sharp grief pangs
From below my skin

Losing or Keeping

I know how to lose people
Did it a million times
You just stay open minded
Keep growing
Evolve and stretch
Reach out in the light
Pluck ideas off branches
Ingest the fruits
Of your search
And let them become
Part of your soul
People will look askance
Repelled and repulsed
Lost them!

I know how to keep people
Did it several times
You just stay open minded
Keep growing
Evolve and stretch
Reach out in the light
Pluck ideas off branches
Ingest the fruits
Of your search
And let them become
Part of your soul
People will look pleased
Come close and embrace
Kept them!

Rag Doll

Years of holding
Your weight
Spineless figure
Propping you up
With those
Weak morals
Feeble character
Shaky willpower
Faulty honesty

No dear, you can't
Be expected
To stand
Upright on
Firm ground
You don't
Possess
The fortitude
The strength
That grows from
Building integrity

You tell me
I'm weak
But you're the one
Who can't sit up
Without me

In the Earth

Some people are like bushes
Branches twined in a thick network
Leaves budding
Berries swelling
Birds nesting
Roots plunging
Each year they reach farther
Taking sun's touch for granted

I'm like a bulb in the earth
Whose stalk is bitten off
Ever trying
Still hoping
Worms slithering
Roots stretching
Each year my shoot devoured
In infancy's first touch of sunlight

Mary Lennox knows the truth
Latent blooms still linger in me
Each year a new prospect
With stronger roots

Is Life Harder Now?

People expect that life gets hard
When you leave your husband,
Five kids in tow
When you're all alone
With a house and the pets
When you can't get help
If the flu lays you flat

People don't know the sigh of relief
When a problem strikes
First the sink pipes burst
When the dog is sick
Then you burn your hand
When he's way across town
And he can't make things worse!

Build a New Normal

Learning to live after resuscitation

Always In My Hands

My hands hold
Things dreamt about
Things sought in battle
Things carefully gathered
In green gardens
In the real world
In this new life
Gems sweetly glistening
Gems inestimable
Gems terribly costly

My hands hold
Words like weapons
Words of condemnation
Words I can't forget
Shards from attacks
Shards that cut deep
Shards of despair
Regret of lost chances
Regrets unassuaged
Regrets deaf to reason

The latter are never
Displaced by the former
They coexist with
The beauty I hold

Worth the Pain?

Is it worth the pain?
The heavy fog of deception
Twisted barbs of abuse
Berated as demonized
Ignored while in pain
Shamed for doubting
Silenced for voicing truth
Labeled rebellious
Despite pure obedience

Resilience was forged
In the hellfire of heresy
Fortitude was grown
In the toil of futility
Gratitude was birthed
In the ache of starvation
Hope was discovered
In the wilderness of rejection
Joy was glimpsed
In the cracks of the walls
Are these worth the pain?
Goodness, no, not one bit

I would rather possess
A mind unprogrammed by deception
A body untouched by trauma
A soul unfamiliar with betrayal

Those would be worth
Innumerable riches
There's no comparison
Between scars and whole flesh
Beauty from ashes
Will never smell like
Wholesome fruit born
In lush orchard fields

Shunned

To you I look like an ogre
A walking spectacle
With sickly heresy
Mind full of lies
Hands spilling blood
Contagious with putrid
Depraved temptations

Even so, I walk upright
A meandering emigrant
With shimmering truth
Mind full of sense
Heart spilling gratitude
Radiating with salvation
Liberated perceptions

Dear Suffering

Dear Suffering,
You brought famine to our home for fifteen years.
Scarcity beyond just food and money
Weakened us with endless, unsolvable problems,
Then ran ahead to our future, stealing any hope of ease.

Dear Suffering,
You tortured our health like a wildfire,
Blazing with fury through our helpless bodies.
Our exhausted, terrified, angry voices cried out
For mercy, begged God to stay your obdurate hand.

Dear Suffering,
You ravaged our relationships like a tornado,
Sweeping people up and away, erratic like a cyclone.
They're blown out of reach by forces too mighty
For our feeble arms to counteract or block.

Dear Suffering,
You devastated our theology like a volcano's blast,
Melting a solid object into charred fragments
Without regard for a lifetime's careful work
Of pressing grand complexities into narrow boxes.

Dear Suffering,
Your inexorable hand wrought these catastrophes,
Brought us to this empty place where grief flows.
Weary and aching, we finally lay down on the battlefield,
Spent from long combat with you, relentless adversary.

Dear Suffering,
In desolation there's unexpected peace and security.
When all is lost, there's nothing left to defend,
No more striving, toiling or guarding property.
The land is waiting for us to rebuild.

The Strong One

I was fine all along!
He told me otherwise,
Pointed out my flaws,
My failures and shame.
I dared to expect things
Like choosing my clothes,
Selecting my friends
And care when I'm sick.
Such blatant indiscretions
Shamed and berated.
I needed his wisdom
To keep me in line.

I was fine all along!
Kindhearted and good,
Fervently working towards
Our family's goals.
The yardstick kept moving,
He never felt pleased -
When I moved a mountain
complained even more.
I felt like a failure.
He put up with me.
But I was the wise one
Who found an escape.

Asher

Your brilliant mind was spinning
From the moment you were born
Deciphering and computing
Restless
Taking in
All the many millions
Of curious data points

Big people are confusing
But you'll learn to crack the code
Of behavior in these humans
Patterns soon
Emerge
Their habits, their intentions
You map out the clues

Sweet boy, there's just one problem
In your growing databank
The humans in your world
Cannot cope
With life
The poorest of examples
Dysfunctional and blind

Your many apprehensions
And the fallout that ensues
Your best laid plans for life
How could you
Succeed
None of them can give you
The map for life you crave

Don't worry, it'll turn up
Late but not too late for you
Before you leave the nest
You will soon
Obtain
New frameworks and good data
To guide you from now on

Peripheral Neuropathy: One of Covid's Gifts

My foot is miles and miles
away from my brain
like a balloon sailing
into the cloudy oblivion.
Can I catch the string?
Reaching, fumbling, teetering . . .

I've caught the string
and my legs stutter
their awkward gait
transporting me across
the floor conspicuously.
How far is it to the chair?

Five steps done but
that darn string is gone,
drifting away again
into the clouds.
This room became ten city blocks;
I'd like a subway to my couch.

Book Choices

My children are
Resilient
Determined
Creative
and
Kind
Curious
Crafty
Engaging
and
Sly
Mischief aplenty
But not all the time
Oh why did I choose to
Read them Roald Dahl?
What may have happened
If I chose instead
Only the Bible
To train their young minds?

Read Aloud Time

Hundreds of drawings
Thousands of words

Three little people
Craning to see

Turning the pages
Breathless delight

Stuffies and blankies
Baby dolls, cars

Giggles erupting
Antics and farce

Misty-eyed blinking
Pathos and fright

Just two more pages
Maybe one more

Avonlea sunset
Dank London fog

Arthur's round table
Laura's log home

Moments so precious
Once commonplace

What was our last book?
Oliver Twist?

Didn't know last time
Was our last time

Life's sudden changes
Swept this away

I'd pay any price now
To revisit those days

Crochet Therapy

Fingers flit
Along each row
Winding yarn
Colors flow
Over, under
Double crochet
Emotions drain
Words I can't say
Frenetic movements
Slow to a hum
Worry fades to
Steady thrum
Hook and fiber
Art I'll wear
Found the flow
My soul's fresh air

Enigma

No easy labels
Affix themselves
To your keen mind
Or mosaic heart
My favorite people
Are label-less

Tangled but flowing
Life force still beating
Starved yet filled
Overflowing, parched
A clear enigma
Nonsensical soul

A spring source within
Replenishes vigor
Sufficient for now
Survive, not thrive
These mundane years
Dusk, never night

Daylight may break
Earth still spins
Might another rotation
Bring spring again?
Rebirth can be found
By mosaic hearts

Solid Ground or Quicksand?

Are you ready to enter full color?
    Ready to see the true truth?
    Ready to leap and discover
    If you hit quicksand
    or firm earth?
Are you ready to stop your daydreaming?
    Ready to leave hazy fog?
    Ready to trade the conjectures
    for a home and hearth,
    solid turf?
Are you ready to be loved forever?
    Ready to see if this might
    persist through all of your seasons?
    Are the gods at play
    with a trap?
Are you ready to love one forever?
    Ready to mend many wounds
    evolving alongside another
    to keep this love strong
    and secure?

Security

Security: a deceptive state
Wherein the rainy day
Is not a fear. How great
And solid seems one's wealth,
Pennies saved and hid
Away for time of need.
Now off come lids
From jars laid aside
When jobs are scarce or health
Grows weak. But have we
Tried a different trust
Giving up of our control
To One who far exceeds
Our scant storehouse. He sends
Fresh provisions into
Our hands if only we
As dependent beings raise
Them up in need.

Anthony

Unsought gift
Unassuming wee thing
Unforeseen blessing

It's not your fault
You arrived in a war zone
You had no choice
But to need our care

My body was broken
Neurological quandary
Did my best to cherish
My sweet Tony Pie

You never encountered
The mom of your siblings
The one able bodied
To raise a whole brood

Your mother can't function
Like others her age do
Still her love envelops
Sweet Anthony Pie

Long Covid

Long Covid, you're too heavy
Like the X-ray blanket
Invisibly hanging off my frame
How do I take you off?

Long Covid, you're too sharp
Like a cruel dagger
Invisibly jabbing my organs
How do I take you out?

Long Covid, you're too hazy
Like a balloon released
Invisibly making my mind float
How do I pin you down?

Long Covid, you're too tingly
Like a machine that's buzzing
Invisibly alarming my nerves
How do I find the off switch?

Long Covid, you're too haphazard
Like a kitten with a new toy
Invisibly pouncing here, then there
How do I make you behave?

My Heart

My heart
Has been parched
Like a dry houseplant
It's been cold
Like my hands
In December wind
Tender in grief
Tenacious with hope
Might it go on
Always
Alive
But dry?

This heart
Feels the warmth
Undeniably here
In your eyes
In your touch
Can't deny this glow
Tender in care
Tenacious with hope
Might it go on
Always
Alive
And bright?

www.ingramcontent.com/pod-product-compliance
Lightning Source LLC
Chambersburg PA
CBHW070735030726
47601CB00001B/27